AMERICAN WRITING AWARDS
FINALIST

NO MORE

A Marriage Devotional

SUFFERING

for the Hard Places

IN SILENCE

Nicole Billups

Enhanced DNA
DEVELOP. NURTURE. ACHIEVE.
Publishing Division

www.EnhancedDNAPublishing.com
DenolaBurton@EnhancedDNA1.com
317-537-1438

No More Suffering in Silence
2021 FINALIST Self-Help – American Writing Awards

Graphic Artist/Cover Design: Marvin Rhodes Jr.
Author Headshots: Kaloma Davis Sr.
Editing: Brock Ferlaak

ISBN-13: 978-1-7369079-4-8
Library of Congress Number: 2021917728

DEDICATION

To my sons KeAndre' Howard and Tyron Bails,
Thank you for always being my motivation to keep going,
no matter what!
You are two of God's greatest blessings in my life!

Nicole Billups

TABLE OF CONTENTS

FOREWORD VII

INTRODUCTION IX

PART I **11**

    ABANDONMENT..13

    ANXIETY 17

    BROKENHEARTED 21

    CAGED 23

    CONDEMNED...27

    DECEPTION 31

    DISRESPECTED 35

    EXHAUSTION 39

    FOOLISH...43

    GRIEF 47

    HOPE...51

    HOSTILITY 55

    LONELINESS 59

PART II **63**

    MANIPULATION..65

    NERVOUSNESS...69

    OVERBEARING 73

    POWERLESSNESS...77

    REJECTION 81

    RESENTMENT 85

    SHAME...89

    TEMPTATION 93

    UNATTRACTIVE...97

    UNLOVED...101

PART III **105**

    UNSTABLE..107

    USED 111

    VIOLATED...115

    WEARY 119

FINAL PRAYER FOR MARRIAGES **123**

ABOUT THE AUTHOR **125**

HELPING HANDS MINISTRIES............................... **127**

Nicole Billups

FOREWORD
By
RoShaunda D. Carpenter

I am super excited about this marriage devotional! I am not surprised at all that God gave Nicole a mission such as this one. She has such a tender heart for God and His people. I believe He called her to write a book of this measure to heal individuals, and their marriages.

As Nicole's pastor and spiritual mother, I have been afforded a front row seat to witness the power of God move through her. I believe it is because of her full reliance on God, that others will be greatly impacted by the movement of Him in her life. This devotional can attest to that!

No More Suffering in Silence, a Marriage Devotional will do more than engage you. Prepare yourself to be challenged in your thinking. Expect this book to increase your capacity to receive from the Holy Spirit. By reading or completing the book, you will be motivated to step out of the way, and fully position yourself for the encouragement and healing that awaits you. With the turn of each page, you are sure to discover that the journey you are on will change your life.

While this is a marriage devotional, I am confident that everyone can benefit from the content of this book, as I'm sure many pastors and servant leaders will agree. It is backed by the Word of God to provide guidance, understanding, and application.

As you navigate through this book, whether alone or with your spouse, allow the Holy Spirit to open your hearts and minds to be mended, delivered and healed!

RoShaunda D. Carpenter
Founder and Senior Pastor- Roaring Fire Ministries
Founder and Leader-The B.E. Free Breakthrough Academy
Indianapolis, Indiana

INTRODUCTION

How many times have you felt alone or betrayed in your marriage? How many times have you wanted to pack things up and walk out, despite the covenant you made with God and your spouse? Although many deny or downplay it to keep up appearances, it happens all the time. I will introduce you to two characters, Renée and Michael, whose struggles in marriage will show us examples of what we might go through when trust and sacred vows are broken.

Are you at a point in your marriage where you are done hearing from others what you should or should not do? No matter how bad things may seem, God is concerned about you and your marriage. He is concerned when you are weary or brokenhearted. He is concerned that you feel abandoned, and He wants you to know that He is right there with you.

If you are tired of suffering behind closed doors while smiling in public, this book is for you. If you are spotting red flags that you missed or thought would go away, this book is for you. If you hoped your love would change your spouse's behavior, this book is for you. Finally, if you are in need of peace in the midst of the storm, this book is for you. Life's circumstances don't always change, but you can be made whole again. I pray that this devotional helps you to heal and inspires you to help others.

Nicole Billups

PART I

"Fear not, for I am with you;
Be not dismayed, for I am your God.
I will strengthen you,
Yes, I will help you,
I will uphold you with My righteous right hand."
                                                    Isaiah 41:10 (NKJV)

Nicole Billups

ABANDONMENT

"Be strong and courageous, do not be afraid or tremble at them, for the LORD your God is the one who goes with you. He will not fail you or forsake you."

Deuteronomy 31:6 (NASB)

Abandonment is one of the worst feelings a person can have during their marriage. The realization that the one who promised before God, family, and friends to be there for you has changed their mind can be emotionally devastating. Renée felt these emotions when she lost her sight during her marriage. One day she woke up with red, painful eyes. Her doctor told her that her optic nerves had swelled to twice the size they should have been. Her vision began to worsen until she could only see shadows. After a myriad of tests and seeing various specialists, she did not have her sight back.

Renée was angry, afraid, and disappointed after every visit to the doctor. She couldn't continue working and had to take a medical leave. In addition, she had to be driven around, could no longer cook her own food, and had to have the names of her medicines read aloud to ensure that she didn't take the wrong ones. At a time when she needed her husband Michael the most, he walked out. She was left heartbroken, afraid, and feeling the most abandoned she had ever felt in her life.

Why would a man who claimed to love her, leave her when she needed him the most? Why would he leave her when she couldn't see? What happened to "through sickness and in health?" She wondered if she did something to make him abandon her. Was it something she said? None of the answers he gave, upon his return, ever made sense to her. However, Renée discovered that when someone abandons you, it is their choice. We all have free will and make our own choices. It has nothing to do with the other individual. Man may leave you, but God never will. He is always by your side and will always make sure you are taken care of, as He did for Renée at her most vulnerable time. God is faithful, and never abandons us!

Reflections: What are your thoughts on **Abandonment**?

_____

_____

_____

_____

_____

_____

_____

_____

_____

_____

_____

_____

_____

_____

_____

_____

_____

Nicole Billups

ANXIETY

"Be anxious for nothing, but in everything by prayer and supplication, with thanksgiving, let your requests be made known to God; and the peace of God, which surpasses all understanding, will guard your hearts and minds through Christ Jesus."

Philippians 4:6-7 (NKJV)

When fear and worry grip you like forceps grip a baby's head during childbirth, you are experiencing anxiety. Merely holding the position of a wife can be a consistent source of anxiety. You could start to worry about whether you are being adequately understanding, compassionate enough, or nagging too much. You might ask yourself questions such as: "Will he like the dinner I prepared?" or "Will there be enough money for the unexpected bills, for home and car repairs?"

The anxiety of being married to someone with an addiction can magnify any other anxiety a wife may be experiencing. This is the type of heightened anxiety that Renée struggled with on a daily basis in her marriage. She worried whether her husband was safe on the nights he left and didn't return home. On his pay days, she worried that he would decide his addiction was more important than helping take care of their bills. Renée often worried that Michael's addiction would cause him to take things from their home. She also worried that his addiction would eventually lead him to commit adultery. Unfortunately, Renée found that her anxiety about many of these situations, turned out to be warranted. Further, she worried every time he left the house at night with their car, that she would have to find a ride to work the next morning.

Anxiety can also be the root of physical illness, and all the worrying began to take a toll on Renée's health. She started experiencing chest pains and increased shortness of breath. The doctors could never find the source of her issues. Her breathing declined rapidly, and she was forced to use oxygen therapy to help her breathe. It wasn't until Renée and Michael briefly separated that her symptoms subsided, and the oxygen was no longer needed. Whatever the current circumstances are in your marriage; please don't allow the anxiety to overwhelm or overtake you. Do what Renée finally decided to do; and put it all in God's hands.

Reflections: What are your thoughts on **Anxiety**?

_____

_____

_____

_____

_____

_____

_____

_____

_____

_____

_____

_____

_____

_____

_____

_____

BROKENHEARTED

"The LORD is near to the brokenhearted And saves those who are crushed in spirit."

Psalms 34:18 (NASB)

A broken heart doesn't suddenly materialize in a marriage. It chips away little by little, as it did for Renée, whose broken heart began two months after she said, "I do." Michael began to show characteristics and traits she hadn't seen during their engagement. During what should have been the honeymoon period, he started staying out all night and entertaining other women. He engaged with them via phone and text like he didn't even have a wife. Four months into the marriage, he quit his job of three years.

Even after acquiring another job, the money fed his addiction more than it helped them take care of their home. With each uncaring act Renée's heart crumbled into pieces. Before she could even recover from the last event, he broke her heart again. She got tired of telling her friends about the awful things that he was doing because she felt foolish and ashamed for staying with him. Renée decided to turn to God for help and for the sake of her sanity. He was the only one who truly understood what she was feeling. When she turned to God, He healed her broken heart piece by piece. He helped her to continue loving her husband while He put the pieces back together again.

Reflections: What are your thoughts on **Brokenhearted**?

_____

_____

_____

_____

_____

_____

_____

_____

_____

_____

_____

_____

_____

_____

CAGED

"How long, O Lord? Will you forget me forever? How long will you hide your face from me? How long must I take counsel in my soul and have sorrow in my heart all day? How long shall my enemy be exalted over me?"

Psalms 13:1-2 (NIV)

Renée had always heard that marriage was not for the faint hearted. She knew that trials and tribulations would come to test not only their faith but possibly their love for one another. However, she was willing to go all-in because she knew they loved each other and thought that alone would be enough. Renée believed that when Michael stood before God and their children and promised to love her like Christ loved the church, he meant it. She also assumed that he understood what being the head of the household meant.

Unfortunately, her assumptions were wrong. This man thought that being the head of household was a license to do whatever he pleased. In his mind, she was supposed to accept his late nights in the streets, his not coming home for days at a time, and being told that she talked too much. Renée was devastated when he would use his paycheck any way he wanted to, and him spending their first wedding anniversary with his friends, leaving her alone all night. Renée woke up one day in the first year of their marriage and felt trapped or caged. She knew God hated divorce and that she didn't have biblical grounds to do so. Therefore, she felt stuck with a man who felt he could usurp control over her.

Renée asked, begged, and pleaded with Michael for them to get counseling. Each time he pridefully declined. She began asking God, "How long?" "How long will you allow this man to mistreat me?" "How long will you just sit by and watch him do these things to me?" What Renée didn't realize was that God was there alongside her the whole time. He was the one who kept her sane and gave her the strength to continue being the godly wife instead of seeking revenge. God held her up with his righteous right hand during their marriage. Focusing on God gave her the freedom she thought she had lost.

Reflections: What are your thoughts on **Caged**?

_____

_____

_____

_____

_____

_____

_____

_____

_____

_____

_____

_____

_____

_____

Nicole Billups

CONDEMNED

"The LORD redeems the soul of His servants. And none of those who take refuge in Him will be condemned."

Psalm 34:22 (ESV)

Within the first couple months of Renée and Michael's marriage, Michael's behavior began to drastically change. She felt more like his conquest instead of his wife. She felt like she was just a checkmark on Michael's bucket list. He didn't feel the need to nurture or put any work into their relationship. Renée felt like an old book that gets put on a shelf and used only as needed. Michael acted as if he were free to go forth and conquer other things. One of those other things happened to be other women.

Once Michael's actions, tone, and speech changed, Renée knew that she had made a mistake. She wished she had listened to her mother, friends, and especially to God. They had all told her that she was making a terrible mistake. She knew she was going to be condemned for life in their marriage because she was disobedient to God. Renée thought this marriage was going to be her eternal punishment because God was angry that she didn't listen to Him. But she was so wrong.

Instead, God showed her love, grace, and mercy. Do not allow the enemy to make you condemn yourself for whatever you did because Romans 8:1 tells us that *"There is no condemnation for those who are in Christ Jesus"*. Go to God, repent, and ask for forgiveness. He will forgive you, as He forgave Renée.

Reflections: What are your thoughts on **Condemned**?

_____

_____

_____

_____

_____

_____

_____

_____

_____

_____

_____

_____

_____

_____

_____

_____

Nicole Billups

DECEPTION

"Do not be deceived: God is not mocked, for whatever one sows, that will he also reap. For the one who sows to his own flesh will from the flesh reap corruption, but the one who sows to the Spirit will from the Spirit reap eternal life."

Galatians 6:6-8 (ESV)

In the second year of Renée and Michael's marriage, Michael divulged that he did not marry her only for love as he had previously claimed. He stated that the main reason he married her was the stability and dependability she would give him. He knew that she would make sure that their bills were paid, so he would always have a roof over his head and access to a car. Further, Michael knew that no matter what he did with his money, Renée would always take care of things. However, at that point in their marriage, he loved her more than he ever had, and claimed he wanted to give their marriage a real try.

As Renée listened to the reasons Michael married her, her heart was shattering to pieces inside her chest. She sat there in disbelief and asked herself, "Did he really just say he married me to use me?... Was this marriage just a ruse for him to get whatever he wanted and allow him to live for free?... Should I do bodily harm to him?" Renée couldn't even process the second half of what he said yet. In her hurt, anger, and disgust, she had to take her broken heart to God.

Her decision wasn't out of love for Michael, but out of love for God and the covenant that she had made with God to remain faithful. Renée remembered that whatever she sowed that season, she would reap. By the end of her inner battle, Renée chose to sow to the Spirit instead of the flesh. After much time, and with God's help she chose to forgive and persevere. It wasn't easy, but with God it was possible.

Reflections: What are your thoughts on Deception?

_____

_____

_____

_____

_____

_____

_____

_____

_____

_____

_____

_____

_____

_____

_____

_____

Nicole Billups

DISRESPECTED

"However, let each one of you love his wife as himself, and let the wife see that she respects her husband."

Ephesians 5:33 (ESV)

Giving yourself up for someone is a sacrifice. It means putting their needs before your own. In Renée's marriage, her husband put his needs first and felt that he was entitled to do so. He felt he could stay out late at night or not come home at all, and she wasn't supposed to ask any questions. In addition, Michael thought he could still hold on to old girlfriends and ex-lovers while passing them off as "friends." He would also invite his family over to stay without consulting Renée. She felt so disrespected in her marriage. In return, Michael's behavior destroyed the respect she had for him.

For Renée, it was hard coming to the realization that she did not respect her husband. She realized that she was acting as her husband's judge and jury. But instead of punishing him, it began to negatively change and punish her. Renée got to a point of where she had to release Michael's judgement to God and work on herself instead. She opened her heart and allowed God in. Only then was she able to forgive, look past her husband's disrespect, become the godly wife God called her to be, and begin to love herself.

Reflections: What are your thoughts on **Disrespected**?

_____

_____

_____

_____

_____

_____

_____

_____

_____

_____

_____

_____

_____

_____

_____

_____

Nicole Billups

EXHAUSTION

"Come to me, all you who are weary and burdened, and I will give you rest. Take my yoke upon you and learn from me, for I am gentle and humble in heart, and you will find rest for your souls."
Matthew 11:28 – 29 (NIV)

Exhaustion was never a word Renée thought she would use pertaining to her marriage. She equated exhaustion with long workdays, lots of housework, and the abundance of homework for her classes. Renée knew everyone said that marriage was hard work, but she thought it was supposed to be two people sharing the load. Her exhaustion began two months into the marriage. It was the first time she noticed that her prince was really a frog. She felt like the goal that her husband needed to accomplish and was now done with. Michael felt there was something greater out in the streets than home with his newlywed wife.

Renée began to reflect his choices upon herself. She went looking inward to try to find what it was she was doing wrong. Did she need to buy new clothes? Did she need to change her hair? Should she cook big meals every day of the week after work and stay up late to finish homework? Should she give the house a deep clean weekly instead of bi-weekly? Renée ran herself senseless trying to do all the above.

However, Michael's actions and behavior did not change. Although he stayed out until whenever he wanted and disrespected her in many other ways, she still loved him and wanted her marriage to work. She began to pray for her marriage and for God to change Michael. Renée was so tired of being mistreated and being there for him when it was apparent that he wasn't interested in being there for her. She desperately wanted to behave like he did. Renée wanted to do the things to Michael that he was doing to her. However, Galatians 6:9 (NIV) told her, *"Let us not become wearying in well doing, for at the proper time we will reap a harvest if we do not give up."* This scripture helped Renée continue to fix his meals, do his laundry, and all her other wifely duties while his behavior never changed. God is our source of strength. We can't control how a spouse behaves, but we can control and will be judged for our responses.

Reflections: What are your thoughts on **Exhaustion?**

_____

_____

_____

_____

_____

_____

_____

_____

_____

_____

_____

_____

_____

_____

_____

Nicole Billups

FOOLISH

"Repay no one evil for evil but give thought to do what is honorable in the sight of all. If possible, so far as it depends on you, live peaceably with all. Beloved, never avenge yourselves, but leave it to the wrath of God, for it is written, 'Vengeance is mine, I will repay, says the Lord.' To the contrary, 'if your enemy is hungry, feed him; if he is thirsty, give him something to drink; for by doing so you will heap burning coals on his head.' Do not be overcome by evil but overcome evil with good."

Romans 12:17-21 (ESV)

In 2002 the singer Ashanti released a single called "Foolish." Renée hadn't really listened to the words until after she began experiencing issues in her marriage. She felt that Ashanti had made that song with her in mind. Every word described how she felt once Michael's behavior and actions changed for the worse. There was a part of her that knew she shouldn't have gotten married, but she had loved and trusted him. She also wanted to make things right in the eyes of God. Renée trusted that he was done with his ex-girlfriend. She trusted that he was ready to settle down like he said he was. She trusted that it would work this time, after all the times they ended the relationship before marrying. Renée knew that she loved Michael and didn't want to be without him. She thought that if they got married everything would work out.

Of course, she was wrong to trust his words instead of his actions. As the marriage continued, she felt extremely foolish for saying "I do." Renée had the expectation that Michael would do a miraculous 180 after they got married. However, with every phone call he made in the other room, late night texts, extended time away from home, and whatever else he felt he had the right to do, she realized just how wrong she had been. Renée desperately wanted to make Michael feel the same pain that he was inflicting upon her. She wanted him to suffer like she was suffering. Renée wanted to walk out of the covenant that she had made with him and God. She wondered how her husband could treat her like he did. She decided to go into deep prayer.

Renée didn't understand how God could continue to allow this man to mistreat her. Did God really expect her to treat him as if he was a great husband? Getting revenge is not God's way. Renée printed out the above scripture and put it in different places in the house to remind herself of God's will for her. She had to learn how to love while she was hurt and feeling more foolish than she ever had in her entire life. Some days, Renée excelled. Then other days she failed miserably. But she decided to get up each day and try all over again because it was what God would have wanted her to do. Renée had to move out of the way and allow God to deal with her husband. Again, God's way is the best way.

Reflections: What are your thoughts on **Foolish?**

_____

_____

_____

_____

_____

_____

_____

_____

_____

_____

_____

_____

_____

Nicole Billups

GRIEF

The LORD is close to the broken hearted and saves those who are crushed in spirit.

Psalm 34:18 (NIV)

He heals the brokenhearted and binds up their wounds.

Psalm 147:3 (NIV)

Grief was a feeling Renée thought she would only feel when her loved ones died. Well, she discovered that grief can be felt at the loss of a person, dream, goal, or a way of life that one had great hopes of living. As her marriage continued, the dream of having a loving, faithful husband seemed to drift further and further out of her reach. The goal of them traveling together seemed impossible because he didn't want to help save money. Renée was a saver and Michael was a spender. Her vision of them growing old together, sitting in rocking chairs on their porch watching their grandchildren play, dissipated with each passing day.

Renée thought, "If only he would change," "If only I had listened to my family and friends," and "If only I had listened to the spirit of God when He told me not to marry Michael." Now here she was, heartbroken and grief stricken. She felt like someone had snatched her heart out of her chest, ran it over with a semi, and then backed up over it at least twenty times. Do you get the picture? She didn't want to go to her friends or family with her grief. She didn't know what to do.

Her heart was shattered into infinite pieces, and she needed help. So, she went to the only person she knew who could help her…God! Renée found the two scriptures above and meditated on them daily. She also reminded God of his promises to heal her broken heart. It wasn't easy to love with a broken heart, but God tells us that, *"I can do all things through him that gives me strength"* Philippians 4:13 (NIV). God gave Renée the strength to love her husband past her pain.

Reflections: What are your thoughts on **Grief**?

_____

_____

_____

_____

_____

_____

_____

_____

_____

_____

_____

_____

_____

_____

_____

_____

_____

Nicole Billups

HOPE

"Oh, that I might have my request, that God will grant what I hope for."

Job 6:8 (NIV)

With the dawn of each new day, Renée hoped it would be better than the day before. She hoped God had heard her cry and things in her marriage would be better. She hoped that they wouldn't argue. She hoped that dinner would be made when she got home from work. He had been home all day and promised to cook for them. She hoped that just maybe Michael would be waiting to spend some time with her instead of waiting to take the keys to the truck as soon as she got home. She hoped that her pain and resentment wouldn't come out as sarcasm.

Each day Renée hoped her husband would see that holding on to his ex-girlfriend was hurting their marriage. She hoped that maybe one day, Michael would listen and apply the godly counsel he consistently received on how to be a godly husband. Renée hoped that she would be able to find a way to fix her marriage. She hoped that if they went to bed together, that he wouldn't get a late- night call or text. She hoped that one day her husband would go into rehab and finish the program. Each day Renée hoped that God would answer her prayers, deliver Michael from his addiction, change him, and make him act right.

However, the more she hoped and prayed for his change, the more she began to change. As Renée kept praying about Michael's issues, God began to reveal her own. The more Renée wanted Michael to be still so she could put the mirror in front of him, the more God continued putting it in front of her.

Her hope for change in her marriage pushed her closer to God. Her hope for a better spouse resulted in her becoming a better person and spouse. It was not her plan, nor did she feel it was needed. But God knows what's needed and will start with the spouse that is willing to let him in. Renée didn't get what she hoped for in her marriage. But she did become a person filled with forgiveness, peace, grace, love, compassion and strength. Never give up hope! You never know where it will lead you.

Reflections: What are your thoughts on **Hope**?

_____

_____

_____

_____

_____

_____

_____

_____

_____

_____

_____

_____

_____

_____

_____

_____

Nicole Billups

HOSTILITY

"Be kind and compassionate to one another, forgiving each other, just as in Christ God forgave you."
Ephesians 4:32 (NIV)

Renee had been called many things in her life, but hostile had never been one of them. She had always had a calm, reserved, friendly demeanor with everyone who knew her. However, somewhere during her marriage, hostility toward her husband became like second nature. Although she knew it was wrong, there were days she wouldn't speak to him out of anger and hurt. Renée knew he was having relationships with other women and was fed up with it. There were days that she would intentionally skip cooking or do things she knew would irritate him. Further, she would purposely stay out in their only car, so Michael couldn't hang out in the streets or go see other women. Renée was angry and hurt so she decided to lash out when she could. At one point she lost all compassion toward him.

Forgiving Michael was not an idea Renée entertained in the beginning, but eventually her hostility caught up to her. She began having chest pains, shortness of breath, and other health issues. Things got so bad that Renée had to wear supplemental oxygen to breathe. The doctors couldn't figure out why it happened, but the Holy Spirit let Renée know the reason. She had to listen to a loud machine in her living room every night as she lay there wondering where Michael was or if he was coming home at all. Her hostility may have been hurting him like she intended, but it was becoming detrimental to her own wellbeing.

Renée was forced to make a crucial decision about her marriage and her health. She knew her failing health was due to her feelings and emotions about her marriage. She realized that she was hurting herself with her unforgiveness and bitterness. Therefore, she began to entertain the thought of forgiving Michael for everything he had done. She struggled with the mere thought of forgiving him. Renée felt that he didn't deserve her forgiveness after all that he had put her through. But then she remembered all that she had put God through, all the disobedience, broken commandments, and times she had disappointed God because of her selfishness. The above scripture helped her to remember that God forgave her while she was deep in her sin. Who was she to not forgive Michael?

Reflections: What are your thoughts on **Hostility?**

_____

_____

_____

_____

_____

_____

_____

_____

_____

_____

_____

_____

_____

_____

_____

Nicole Billups

LONELINESS

"When you pass through the waters, I will be with you; and when you pass through rivers, they will not sweep over you. When you walk through the fire, you will not be burned; the flames will not set you ablaze. For I am the LORD your God, the Holy One of Israel, your Savior; I give Egypt for your ransom, Cush and Seba in your stead."
Isaiah 43:2-3 (NIV)

Loneliness is something Renée never thought she would feel as a married woman. In fact, she thought marriage was going to be one of the solutions to her loneliness. She thought she had finally found the ultimate solution to her lifelong feeling of loneliness. She thought she had found her best friend who would be with her no matter the day or circumstance. It was supposed to be Michael and Renée against the world. He was going to be her Superman and she was going to be his Lois Lane. She would never again feel like she didn't fit in. She thought that she finally had someone who loved and accepted her with all her flaws.

Unfortunately, throughout their marriage it never managed to be just the two of them. Eighty-five percent of the time Renée came in last place to the streets, other women, or drugs. She spent more time alone as a married woman than she did as a single woman. The next thing was always more important to Michael. We could talk later. We could spend time together later. We could catch up on date night next week. There was always some type of fool's gold that took his attention away from Renée and their marriage.

One day Renée decided to go to her Abba Father for comfort and help. He became her secret keeper. She prayed, cried, and sometimes both for months. She knew that He wouldn't judge her for staying or for continuing to love her husband in spite of his actions and behavior toward her. Renée didn't get married to get divorced. She loved her husband and wanted her marriage to work. God helped her to see that she was not alone. He was there to hear, comfort, and heal her. Deuteronomy 31:6 (NIV) told Renée to *"Be strong and courageous. Do not be afraid or terrified because of them, for the LORD your God goes with you; he will never leave nor forsake you."* She clung to this scripture for dear life. It helped her to feel a little less lonely. She was still hurt, but no longer alone.

Reflections: What are your thoughts on Loneliness?

_____

_____

_____

_____

_____

_____

_____

_____

_____

_____

_____

_____

_____

_____

_____

_____

Nicole Billups

PART II

"God is our refuge and strength,
A very present help in trouble."
                              Psalm 46:1 (KJV)

Nicole Billups

MANIPULATION

"It is for freedom that Christ has set us free. Stand firm, then, and do not let yourselves be burdened again by a yoke of slavery."
Galatians 5:1 (NIV)

One definition of manipulate is "to handle, manage, or use." This is exactly what Renée endured. She thought she was doing things she didn't want to do out of love, when in fact, it was out of manipulation. Who would think that the spouse who promised to love and cherish you through sickness and in health, till death do you part would even think about attempting to manipulate you? Unfortunately, it happens. However, Renée allowed the manipulation in part because she didn't have her own identity. She allowed Michael to manipulate her with his words and deeds. In addition, her self-esteem was extremely low, and she just wanted to be loved. She thought that if she did almost everything he asked of her, she would get the love she had always wanted.

Renée thought that she would no longer have to be in competition with other women or drugs. She gave him gas money so he could run the streets after he went on and on about not being able to go anywhere because she had the car all day at work. But Michael had no job to go to and would return the car on empty. Renée would then have to fill another tank so she could get to work. Further, there would be jobs that he would just walk out of because he didn't like the way they spoke to him. Michael convinced Renée that he would have a job by the next week to deter her concern. However, there would always be a sickness or illness that kept him on the couch watching tv while she headed out to work. She finally got tired of it!

Renée got closer to God and got into therapy. The better and stronger she got; the more upset Michael became. He noticed that his manipulation didn't work as easily and finally not at all. He could no longer benefit from her dysfunction. God delivered Renée from manipulation. He can deliver you as well. Manipulation is not of God. Trust God to heal and deliver you as well.

Reflections: What are your thoughts on **Manipulation**?

_____

_____

_____

_____

_____

_____

_____

_____

_____

_____

_____

_____

_____

_____

Nicole Billups

NERVOUSNESS

"When I am afraid, I put my trust in you."
Psalm 56:3 (NIV)

During her marriage, "What if" became something Renée spoke or thought of daily. "What if Michael gets paid and decides to get high instead of helping pay the bills? What if he leaves and stays out all night? What if he's texting his ex-girlfriend instead of his daughter like he said he was? What if he clears out our house while I'm at work and goes on a drug binge? What if he takes the car and pawns it for drugs and I can't get to work? What if I don't have enough to cover all of the bills and food because he spent his check getting high and having fun?" These are just a sample of questions that ran through Renée's mind on a regular basis.

She was nervous whenever she had to depend on him to do anything. Michael had a proven track record of being unreliable in their marriage. Renée felt like she was always on pins and needles. She never knew what the next day would bring. There always seemed to be a situation that took more from her sanity than it should have. Finally, she decided that enough was enough. She knew that she couldn't change him, so she had to change her reactions. Only God could help her to do that.

Although her husband's actions didn't change, Renée's reactions did. She was able to sleep with or without his presence. She was able to focus on her job and help others. She decided to feed her faith and starve her fear. Renée knew that her sanity was at stake, and she refused to allow Michael to continue to cause her to lose it. She decided to trust God no matter what her husband did or said. She allowed God to be responsible for Michael, not her. Allow God to fight your battles in your marriage. It will bring you peace and restore your joy as it did for Renée.

Reflections: What are your thoughts on **Nervousness**?

Nicole Billups

OVERBEARING

"My dear brothers and sisters, take note of this: Everyone should be quick to listen, slow to speak and slow to become angry, because human anger does not produce the righteousness that God desires."
James 1:19-20 (NIV)

Overbearing was a word that Renée's husband used quite often to describe her during their marriage. Michael made a point of letting her know how bossy and domineering he felt she was in the relationship. At first, Renée attributed it to him being upset when she didn't allow him to have his way. Later, she didn't care because she was walking around hurt, bitter, and angry due to the constant disrespect from him. Renée had been raised by a single mother who taught her to stand on her own two feet and to never trust a man for anything. Then, she became a single mother of three and found out that there were at least two men who fit her mother's theory. Therefore, Renée thought that her mother had been correct. She decided that she would work to take care of her children and, as her mother would say, "Pay the cost to be the boss." Well ladies, this is NOT the right attitude to have in a marriage.

There can only be one head in a marriage. Regardless of how the head is behaving; there can only be one head and that's the husband. Imagine a two headed monster where both heads are moving and biting each other to remove the other and take their rightful position. Anything with two heads is distorted and will not work properly. They will always compete and vie for leadership over the other. This is exactly what happened in Renée and Michael's marriage. Renée admitted that she went into her marriage with the wrong mindset. She used her husband's behavior as an excuse to be overbearing and controlling. Renée felt that she had to protect herself from the continual pain, instead of allowing God to do so. Ephesians 5:33 (NIV) tells us, *"However, each one of you must also love his wife as he loves himself, and the wife must respect her husband."* Further, she used her husband's behavior as her reason to disrespect him as a person and the head of their home.

Once her blinders were removed, Renée repented and saw the error of her ways. We must realize that we are each responsible for our actions as well as our reactions. We must trust God to do and be who he says he is in our marriage. We must give him the reins without taking them back from him. Let every one of your actions and reactions exhibit God's character.

Reflections: What are your thoughts on **Overbearing?**

Nicole Billups

POWERLESSNESS

"The LORD gives strength to his people; the LORD blesses his people with peace."

Psalm 29:11 (NIV)

Imagine waking up in a black hole. There is no ladder to climb out and you see no other way of escaping. Furthermore, there are unseen traps in the hole that you can't defend yourself from. So here you are, at the mercy of the black hole and whatever it's traps will do to you. This is how Renée felt in her marriage. She felt powerless over the mistreatment that she received from Michael. She couldn't stop or change it. She couldn't make him love her in the same way that Christ loves the church.

Renée couldn't make him spend more time with her, value their marriage as much as she did, or participate in marriage counseling. Further, Renée couldn't divorce him because he was staying all night, getting high, or spending his money frivolously. She wanted things to be different because she loved Michael with all her heart. She wanted to have that love that she had heard and dreamed about. Renée wanted the forever love she thought only her husband would be able to give her.

In the end, she found herself completely powerless to change another human being. Guess what? Changing another person is not our job. God is the only one who can change the heart of man. Jesus said, *"I will give you a new heart and put a new spirit in you; I will remove from you your heart of stone and give you a heart of flesh"* Ezekiel 36:26 (NIV). Sooner or later, we must realize that we are not the Messiah. When we are weak, He is made strong. When you begin to feel powerless in your marriage, give it over to the one who holds all power in His hands.

Reflections: What are your thoughts on **Powerlessness**?

_____

_____

_____

_____

_____

_____

_____

_____

_____

_____

_____

_____

_____

Nicole Billups

REJECTION

"The righteous cry out, and the LORD hears them; he delivers them from all of their troubles. The LORD is close to the brokenhearted and saves those who are crushed in spirit. The righteous person may have many troubles, but the LORD delivers him from them all; he protects all of his bones, not one of them will be broken."
Psalm 34: 17-20 (NIV)

Rejection can come in many forms, in many areas and from many different people. But to experience rejection from the man she loved was earth shattering for Renée. She thought that she had found her Prince Charming. She thought this spontaneous, romantic man who had been her best friend, confidant, tear dryer, and shoulder to lean on was "him." He brought her flowers just because. He loved to take walks or car rides just to enjoy her company, called several times a day to check in on how she was doing, and soothed her during rough times. Michael seemed as if he could never get enough of her. She knew from the bottom of her heart that this man would never reject her. Yet she was wrong.

When they got married, his once charming behavior drastically changed. She was devastated! Renée thought that she had woken up in an alternate universe one morning. Almost everything else became more important to Michael than she was. This may have been the hardest rejection she had ever faced. She felt extremely hurt, disappointed and alone. She began wondering what she had done to make him change, and why the change had occurred after they got married. All she had was a bunch of unanswered questions.

However, she also had God with her. He is the one who never leaves nor forsakes us. He is the one who has *"chosen us in him before the creation of the world to be holy and blameless in his sight"* Ephesians 1:4 (NIV). We are chosen by the King of Kings and the Lord of Lords! We are precious in His sight. No matter at whose hands we may suffer rejection, there is a God who will never reject us. There is a God who hasn't changed his mind about choosing us and no matter the circumstance, He never will.

Reflections: What are your thoughts on Rejection?

_____

_____

_____

_____

_____

_____

_____

_____

_____

_____

_____

_____

_____

_____

_____

_____

_____

Nicole Billups

RESENTMENT

"But if you do not forgive others their sins, your Father will not forgive your sins."

Matthew 6:15 (NIV)

Somewhere in Renée's marriage, resentment became her best friend. Renée became more loyal and faithful to resentment than she was to being a godly wife for Michael. She had become so tired of the lies, loneliness, deceit, manipulation, and everything else that he was doing. Renée thought that she had finally found a true friend in resentment. Resentment wouldn't disappoint her and would always be there when she needed him. By the end of the first year of her marriage resentment and Renée were besties.

Oftentimes, she tried to hide her bestie from outsiders and family, but her actions toward Michael would usually show that he was there. However, Renée failed to realize that her bestie was doing her and their marriage more harm than good. She allowed her bestie to have his way daily. She felt that she was justified in allowing resentment to take over. When her bestie took over, Renée didn't have to feel so vulnerable to the mistreatment she was receiving. She walked around with her head held high as if she had never done anything wrong, or at least it wasn't equivalent to Michael's sin. She wanted her husband closer, but her resentment pushed him farther away.

We must be careful what and who we allow into our marriages. Yes, we are allowed to be angry about situations, but we should not allow any negative emotion to continually influence our behavior toward our spouse. Further, we shouldn't think more highly of ourselves than we ought to. Romans 12:3 (NIV) tells us *"For by the grace given me I say to everyone of you: do not think of yourself more highly than you ought, but rather think of yourself with sober judgment, in accordance with the faith God has distributed through each of you."* Think back to all that you have done wrong. If God can forgive you, then you can forgive your spouse. In great marriages, forgiveness is a daily choice.

Reflections: What are your thoughts on **Resentment**?

_____

_____

_____

_____

_____

_____

_____

_____

_____

_____

_____

_____

_____

_____

_____

Nicole Billups

SHAME

"Instead of your shame you will receive a double portion, and instead of disgrace you will rejoice in your inheritance. And so, you will inherit a double portion in your land, and everlasting joy will be yours."
Isaiah 61:7 (NIV)

No matter how much encouragement Renée got or how many worship and praise songs she heard or sermons she listened to, she still felt an abundance of shame regarding her marriage to Michael. Renée felt an overwhelming shame because of the choice she made in a spouse and the unwanted life that came with it. She felt shame because the Spirit of the Lord told her not to marry Michael, but she was disobedient. In the beginning she thought maybe she deserved the mistreatment because she didn't listen to God.

Renée was ashamed of herself because she knew better and was ashamed of the way she was being treated in her marriage. She was ashamed that they were unequally yoked, and yet she entered it with her eyes wide open to this. She couldn't believe that she had married a man who had infidelity, substance abuse issues, and a poor work ethic before they got married! Renée wondered if she was desperate, lonely, or both. She wasn't proud to admit that Michael was her new husband like most new brides are. The shame became evident in her husband's eyes. Nothing she could do in her own strength changed the way she felt.

A dear friend pointed her toward Christ for help. Once she saw how severely she was hurting Michael, she knew she needed God to help her. Renée couldn't change her thinking on her own. She went to God and repented for her disobedience, and then asked God to help her to see her husband through His eyes rather than her own. She had a heart problem that only God could fix. She may have made a mistake, but she didn't have to continue condemning herself or her husband for it. In light of her husband's actions, she needed God to rid her of her shame so that she could love and respect her husband as God commanded her to do. It was a process. But with God. Renée got there and you can too.

Reflections: What are your thoughts on **Shame**?

_____

_____

_____

_____

_____

_____

_____

_____

_____

_____

_____

_____

_____

_____

Nicole Billups

TEMPTATION

"Dear friends, do not be surprised at the fiery ordeal that has come on you to test you, as though something strange were happening to you."
1 Peter 4:12 (NIV)

Renee declared that she could still remember the day that she began feeling tempted to go outside of her marriage for relief. Michael had apologized for selling their $500 snow tires to get money to get high. She had just bought tires for the Spring and the snow tires were supposed to stay in the garage until the next Winter. Not only did he sell them, but he continued lying about it. Renée was still trying to deal with another episode from the prior week. She was feeling overwhelmed, disrespected, hurt, angry, and was losing respect for him as each episode of drama occurred. God saw what was going on, and so did the devil.

She began getting calls from an ex-boyfriend. It was nice to hear sweet things for a change. It was nice to talk instead of arguing for once. It was nice to get "Good Morning Beautiful" text messages from someone who wasn't lying, stealing, or emotionally abusing her. The phone calls and text messages became more frequent over the next several weeks following the tire incident. Renée felt it was also easier to deal with her husband's issues and being left alone at home so much with an outside emotional attachment. Although she knew in her heart that it was wrong and could lead her to where a married woman shouldn't go, she continued.

Finally, her ex-boyfriend asked to meet her at a hotel. A big part of her was truly tempted to go and be with him. She felt she deserved it after all her husband had been doing. But the other part of her knew that no matter what Michael was doing, for her to go would be wrong. She had made a covenant with God and her husband, for better or for worse. Renée couldn't believe that she had even contemplated it. She was too ashamed to tell anyone, so she sat, prayed and listened.

God showed her that she opened the door to temptation by talking to that man. The enemy was using that man at the right time to destroy their marriage. Renée had to make a choice to either forgive Michael and keep fighting for their marriage or give up and dive into sin. She chose her marriage. Renée cut off all communication with her ex and worked on forgiving her husband the way God forgives her. *"We must not be ignorant of the enemy's devices"* 2 Corinthians 2:11, (NIV). The enemy will use anything and anyone to destroy your marriage. When you are tempted to do anything that will hurt, disrespect, or take away from your marriage, allow God to make a way of escape for you.

Reflections: What are your thoughts on **Temptation**?

_____

_____

_____

_____

_____

_____

_____

_____

_____

_____

_____

_____

_____

_____

_____

Nicole Billups

UNATTRACTIVE

"For you formed her inward parts; you knitted me together in her mother's womb. I praise you, for I am fearfully and wonderfully made. Your works are wonderful, I know that full well."

Psalm 139:13-14 (NIV)

As the nights that Renée spent alone increased, she began to look within herself for the problem and the solution. The first place she started was her outward appearance. She assumed her husband no longer loved what he saw like he did the day he promised to love and cherish her. Surely this was the reason he stayed out late or all night. Surely this was the reason he was romantically talking to other women. She felt that this must have been the reason Michael was keeping naked pictures on his phone that his ex-girlfriend sent him one month after they got married. She felt ashamed for looking in his phone. But this is what a wife does who feels insecure and unattractive. At least, this is what she did.

She began doubting and disliking everything about herself and he told her that it was her issue, not his. When other people gave Renée compliments, she couldn't receive them. She wondered how these people could think that she was beautiful when the one she loved didn't seem to think so. Renée felt that if Michael thought so, he would be with her instead of other women. This distorted thinking led her to feeling ugly, unwanted, down, and depressed. She allowed her husband's actions to make her forget who God says she is. Renée allowed her husband's hurts, habits, and hang ups to become her own. You must remember that you are responsible for your own actions and behavior, not your spouse's. No matter what they do or don't do, you are fearfully and wonderfully made. This fact will never change because God does not change, and He is our creator.

Reflections: What are your thoughts on **Unattractive**?

_____

_____

_____

_____

_____

_____

_____

_____

_____

_____

_____

_____

_____

_____

_____

_____

UNLOVED

"'Though the mountains be shaken, and the hills be removed, yet my unfailing love for you will not be shaken nor my covenant of peace be removed,' says the LORD, who has compassion on you."
Isaiah 54:10 (NIV)

As they pulled up to the library on Saturday, Michael and Renée did not want to part. They had a wonderful morning, but she had to finish a school project. Michael was to return to the library in a few hours to pick her up. As she began to work, the Holy Spirit began to tell her that she should have her husband come back and pick her up. She ignored the Holy Spirit at first because she thought that maybe she was just missing him and wanted to be back in his presence, but she heard it repeatedly. Renée then called Michael to pick her back up. To her surprise, Michael was extremely irritated when she told him that she needed him to return to pick her up. He began raising his voice angrily on the phone. When he arrived his irritation and anger were written all over his face.

After she got in the car, Michael began to argue that he never gets to do what he wants and that she controls everything. The argument ensued between them. He gave Renée a look that she had never seen before. It was beyond anger, but she wasn't sure what it was. He slammed on the breaks twice in the middle of a busy street. Renée was frightened but tried not to let it show. He was driving erratically and said that he would kill them both. She threatened to call the police if he didn't stop immediately. She reached for her purse to get her phone, but Michael started wrestling her for it while driving. He threatened to throw her purse out of his open window.

Thankfully, Renée managed to dial 911. The operator stayed on the phone with her until Michael pulled the car over and got out and began to walk away. Renée's heart was pounding so hard she thought it was going to pop out of her chest. After she hung up, she just sat there and cried her eyes out. She wondered how her husband could risk her life and try to hurt her. She just sat there in disbelief. She wondered if Michael hated her so much that he would try to take her life. Renée could barely see to drive home because her tears would not stop flowing. No matter what Michael did or didn't do, she thought that she would always be able to count on him to love her.

That day Renée found out that an addict's first love is their drug of choice, not their spouse. If one comes between them and their first love, the consequences could possibly prove fatal. She also learned that the only one that she can absolutely count on to always love her is God. God would never love her in the morning and attempt to take her life in the afternoon. God's love is stable and unfailing. God's love gave Renée the strength to continue loving and praying for her husband after that incident and their following time apart.

Reflections: What are your thoughts on **Unloved**?

_____

_____

_____

_____

_____

_____

_____

_____

_____

_____

_____

_____

_____

_____

PART III

"Come to Me, all you who labor and are heavy laden, and I will give you rest. Take My yoke upon you and learn from Me, for I am gentle and lowly in heart, and you will find rest for your souls. For My yoke is easy and My burden is light."

Matthew 11:28-30 (ESV)

Nicole Billups

UNSTABLE

"Submit yourselves, then, to God. Resist the devil, and he will flee from you."

James 4:7 (NIV)

Imagine yourself on the first hill of a rollercoaster. Just as you get slightly comfortable with the ride ascending to a point…it instantly descends. The ups and downs continue throughout the ride until it comes to its final stop. Your heart races as you hold on for dear life and regret your decision to get on the ride in the first place. However, as you get unbuckled and out of the seat, you realize that you somewhat enjoyed the ride and may want to do it again. This mental instability is much like Renée's thoughts during most of her marriage until she decided to submit to God.

One day she was in love with her husband and wanted to do everything she could to be a godly wife and please him. However, once he did something wrong or disrespectful, she put up an impenetrable emotional wall. She didn't want to talk, answer any questions, or pray with him. She dismissed his thoughts and feelings about anything and everything. Renée completely disregarded God's command to love and respect her husband and felt that she was justified in doing so. Renée allowed the enemy to use her to tear down her husband more than the world was already doing. She knew in her heart and spirit that her actions were wrong, but her mind didn't care.

Renée was tired of being mistreated and was going to take back control, or so she thought. Then, she decided that she would start to act half-righteously. She would love, but she would not respect Michael. She would make a meal, but she wouldn't take his plate to him like she used to. She finally realized that all of that was foolishness in the eyes of God. Either you are going to be a godly wife or you're not. Either you are walking in forgiveness or you're not. You are either going to allow God to be the avenger of sin or try to do it yourself.

Attempting to live on both sides of the fence is unstable. Submitting to God while being mistreated by your spouse is no easy feat. Renée was angry and cried bitter tears for months. She asked God why she had to be the one to submit when he was the one doing the most wrong. God reminded her that sin is sin. Every time she put up the emotional wall and acted as if he wasn't there, she disrespected him and was walking in sin. A wife disrespecting her husband is just as sinful as a husband romantically talking to other women. A marital sin is a marital sin. God's work had to start with the spouse that was willing to allow Him in. One can't be double-minded in their marriage and expect God to bless it.

Reflections: What are your thoughts on Unstable?

_____

_____

_____

_____

_____

_____

_____

_____

_____

_____

_____

_____

_____

_____

_____

_____

Nicole Billups

USED

"Do not repay anyone evil for evil. Be careful to do what is right in the eyes of everyone. If it is possible as far as it depends on you, live at peace with everyone. Do not take revenge, my dear friends, but leave room for God's wrath. For it is written: 'It is mine to avenge; I will repay', says the Lord."

Romans 12:17-19 (NIV)

One night about 16 months into their marriage, Renée heard one of the most hurtful, honest things Michael had ever said. He decided to apologize for marrying her for the wrong reason. Imagine Renée's heartache after hearing that the man she loved primarily married her for her stability and the things he thought that she could provide for him. Michael told Renée that he had always loved her, but love wasn't the main reason he married her. She was devastated, and tears welled up in her eyes. The very reason she had married him was not at the top of his list of reasons he married her. He decided that he wanted to be honest because he had fallen deeper in love with Renée and wanted to start over, or so he said.

Michael continued telling her that he knew she always paid her bills, always had a roof over her head, she didn't engage in recreational drugs or alcohol, like he did. He would have a car to drive, and no matter what she would never allow anything or anyone to come before our bills were paid. He said he knew he would always have a lock to turn his key and be comfortable.

Renée began thinking back over the previous 16 months and realized why he had behaved the way he did. The times he had her meet him at a car lot and motorcycle dealership, in hopes that she would purchase either one for him, the times he would spend his paychecks on whatever he wanted without helping with bills, etc. It all now made sense to her. Renée was flabbergasted and didn't know what to think or do. But they decided to work through it.

Michael claimed he would begin to help her with bills, groceries, etc. going forward. It was short lived. Renée couldn't count on him to consistently help her throughout the rest of the marriage. She continued to feel used most of the time. However, Renée tried her best not to allow that feeling to influence her love and behavior toward him. She didn't get it perfect, but with God's help Renée did her best. We must let God be our protector and He will fight our battles, especially in a marriage.

Reflections: What are your thoughts on **Used**?

_____

_____

_____

_____

_____

_____

_____

_____

_____

_____

_____

_____

_____

_____

_____

Nicole Billups

VIOLATED

"The Lord is my shepherd: I shall not want. He makes to lie down in green pastures; He leads me beside still waters. He restores my soul; He leads me in the paths of righteousness for His name's sake. Yea, though I walk through the valley of the shadow of death, I will fear no evil; For you are with me; Your rod and Your staff, they comfort me.

You prepare a table before me in the presence of my enemies; You anoint my head with oil; My cup runs over. Surely goodness and mercy shall follow me All the days of my life; And I will dwell in the house of the LORD forever."

Psalm 23 (NKJV)

With every personal item taken, sold, or pawned, Renée's feeling of violation increased. They say it's a thin line between love and hate. Renée thought she was on her way to crossing over the line to hate when Michael took her schoolbooks and sold them to a college bookstore to get money for his drug addiction. She didn't discover it until the end of her last semester when looking for a reference book to complete her final project. After looking everywhere, she asked her husband if he had seen the book. Michael lied and told her no. He even got up and joined her in her search for it. Renée began looking for other books and didn't find them either. She thought she was losing her mind. She then remembered that Michael had accompanied her to the bookstore when she sold a book she didn't need. Renée had believed that Michael wouldn't take the books that she would need in her field, the ones that she had paid thousands of dollars for. She was angry with him for selling the tires to their truck, her old cell phone, the movies she had bought, some of her Rhythm & Blues CDs, unopened Bath and Body Works products, and even one of her unopened birthday gifts. But her books?! Renée was livid.

Only God was able to give her the peace that she needed to continue being his wife. It was God alone who healed and changed her heart and helped her to forgive and continue in her marriage. She had to remember that God was her shepherd and was able to replace and give her better things than those that Michael took from her. God helped Renée to realize that it was the addiction, and not her husband that was making her feel violated. Although things were taken God was still with her and provided for her throughout the marriage and He will provide for you as well.

Reflections: What are your thoughts on **Violated?**

_____

_____

_____

_____

_____

_____

_____

_____

_____

_____

_____

_____

_____

_____

_____

Nicole Billups

WEARY

"Come to me, all you are weary and burdened, and I will give you rest."

Matthew 11:28 (NIV)

Although Renée continued to smile and appear happy, she wasn't. Her spirit looked like an old, bent over woman who kept her head down as she walked. She had been dragged, pushed, and stressed out to the point of exhaustion. Her family was in shambles. Her husband, Michael, felt he was entitled to his position but didn't want to do the duties that the position required. Renée's grown son hated watching her be mistreated and disrespected. He secretly wished her husband was gone. Her husband publicly wished her son was gone. However, her son was afraid to leave her alone in the house with Michael. He had witnessed the shouting matches and there were times he had to help care for Renée because Michael walked out for days at a time.

Michael felt like Renée was putting her son in his place. She may have done so because her son was there for her when he wasn't. Her son didn't complain about doing things for her that she couldn't do when she was ill. She was so tired of her husband being jealous of her son. God was the only one who gave Renée strength to keep going. She knows that it was only by the grace of God that she stayed sane. When you are weary in your marriage, look to God for strength. Do not step outside of your marriage for anything. God promises to be everything that you need Him to be. Trust Him to do just that.

Reflections: What are your thoughts on **Weary**?

_____

_____

_____

_____

_____

_____

_____

_____

_____

_____

_____

_____

_____

Nicole Billups

FINAL PRAYER FOR MARRIAGES

Most Gracious Heavenly Father, I come to you as humbly as I know how, lifting up every marriage on this side of heaven. Father God, I ask that you give each spouse faith, compassion, and understanding for one another. Lord, your word says to *"Bear with each other and forgive one another if any of us has a grievance against someone, and to forgive as the Lord has forgiven us"* Colossians 3:13 (NIV).

Lord God, I ask that you give each spouse the strength to do just that in your name's sake. Father, help them to remember the reason they started in hope that they will not quit. Help them, Oh God, to *"Submit to one another out of reverence for Christ"* Ephesians 5:21 (NIV). Lord, your word says that *"Love is patient, love is kind. It does not envy, it does not boast, it is not proud. It does not dishonor others, it is not self-seeking, it is not easily angered, it keeps no records of wrongs. Love does not delight in evil but rejoices with the truth. It always protects, always trusts, always hopes, always perseveres. Love never fails. But where there are prophecies, they will cease; where there are tongues, they will be stilled; where there is knowledge, it will pass away"* 1 Corinthians 13:4-8 (NIV).

Lord God, I ask that you help each spouse to learn to love each other in this manner. Father God, have your way in all marriages. Bind them closer than they have ever been before and help them to keep their marriages sacred and holy. Protect their minds, Oh God, from the tricks and schemes of the enemy during challenging times.

Help them to see that it is the enemy they need to fight, and not each other. Father God, do what only you can do, change minds and heal broken hearts. Lord, you said, *"Therefore what you have joined together, let no one separate"* Mark 10:9 (NIV). I ask you in the name of Jesus to cover each marital covenant with your blood, that it not be broken unless you do it. In Jesus Name, Amen!

ABOUT THE AUTHOR

Nicole Billups is a native of Indianapolis, Indiana. She is the mother of two wonderful adult sons, a beautiful daughter-in-love, and a proud grandmother of two beautiful grand-daughters. She has received her Bachelor of Science in Psychology from Martin University, her Master of Arts in Human Services Counseling and Marriage & Family Therapy from Liberty University. She is also currently working on her Master of Arts in Christian Ministry.

Nicole also received her diploma, advanced diploma, and advanced certificate in Biblical Counseling from Light University. She graduated from Authentic Identity Institute as a Certified Christian Life Coach/Human Behavior Consultant with a 5D and DISC certification.

Currently, Nicole is a member of the Roaring Fire Ministries Church, where she is the pastor's armor-bearer and the head of women's ministry. As an inspirational speaker, she has spoken to young girls in the Indiana Juvenile Detention Center and an Indiana Public Schools afterschool girls' group.

In a local ministry, Nicole led a team that ministered to survivors of domestic violence in the Julian Center for Battered Women. Her service included facilitation of small group bible studies, one-on-one mentoring, and biblical counseling.

Nicole has served as a peer counselor for the Life Centers (formally known as the Crisis Pregnancy Center). She has always possessed a servant's heart and a passion for helping and encouraging others.

Nicole Billups

HELPING HANDS MINISTRIES

https://helpinghandsministriesllc.org
helpinghandsmcc@gmail.com
765-734-7188

Helping Hands Ministries was founded out of a desire to see God's people set free from the pain of their past. We aim to help them find their true identity and successfully venture into their purpose.

Vision: To exhibit the love of Christ and to help others overcome their past and present pain; empowering them to take the next step in life.

Mission: Use the Word of God to equip others with Kingdom tools to grow emotionally, mentally, and spiritually, including sustaining a life of freedom.

Services Offered:
- Biblical One on One Mentoring
- Life Coaching
- Human Behavior Consultation (DISC Personality Profile – Assessment & Summary)
- DISC Personality Profile/Spiritual Gift Assessments and Summary
- 5D Workshops
- Inspirational Speaking
- Small Group Bible Studies
- Grief Counseling
- Post Abortive Healing
- Women's Fellowship
- Domestic Violence Conqueror Conferences and more…

Nicole Billups

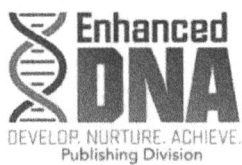

www.ingramcontent.com/pod-product-compliance
Lightning Source LLC
Chambersburg PA
CBHW051430090426
42737CB00014B/2896